COMMON SENSE 2020

An Appeal to the People of the United States of America

JASON D. MEININGER

"To each there comes in their lifetime a special
moment when they are figuratively tapped on the
shoulder and offered the chance to do a very special
thing, unique to them and fitted to their talents. What
a tragedy if that moment finds them unprepared or
unqualified for that which could have been their finest
hour."

— SIR WINSTON CHURCHILL

CONTENTS

❧ I ❧

THE STATE OF AFFAIRS

A moment has come where we possess a duty to remind ourselves of the spirit of our Founding Fathers and Mothers of the United States. As we possess the ability to recognize the decay of our nature, we also possess a natural ability to modernize our Democratic Republic through understanding our history.

Through my commitment to provide public service from history, in comparative politics and through domestic and international affairs, it is my inherent duty as a free, natural citizen, to call for a reclamation of our rights as citizens. From an intent to generate an evolution out of our current problem set, it is imperative we look into the current state of affairs from the outside - in; with a big picture mentality for the future of our country, and our future world.

At this time in our Nation's history, it is as necessary to remember the nature of Publius (*of the people*) through which the 1787 Federalist Papers were anonymously published to explain and justify ratification of the United States Constitution. As much as I would prefer to write this anonymously, it is necessary in today's modern world, to claim authorship and responsibility. To be truly honest, I did not want to have to write this first portion at all, and the latter for another 30 years.

With my Freedom of Speech protected by our First Amendment, the following statements are free from direct political, corporate persuasion, or monetary influence outside of my own savings. Outside the lessons of history, these contents are based on my independently minded experiences.

In 1776 Thomas Paine anonymously published Common Sense which justified cause and reason to our inalienable rights exhibited in the 1776 Declaration of Independence. Through his publication, Thomas Paine intended to create a separation from British rule over the colonies, and began a revolution in doing so.[1] To be clear, the following is intended to promote Peaceful Evolution so we can exercise peaceful elections meant to serve as an evolution from the violent American and French revolutions 1776-1799. Going into the heat of this election season, and through the post-election transition period, we remember our founding fathers designed our election process to guarantee civilization the ability change government through elections as necessary.

In 2020, two hundred and forty-five years after Thomas Paine wrote the original Common Sense, another encourage-ment to practice Common Sense is necessary. As we face similar constraints and interferences to the service American freedom has promised to provide through the preservation of liberty the pursuit of happiness, we are one America in trou-ble. Free from the entangling alliances warned of in President George Washington's 1796 Farewell Address, we must vote for our future like never before and without interference from foreign or domestic entanglements. The freedom intended for our electoral process is at stake until we exercise our freedom of choice to vote.

The best interests of the American public have become

not only misrepresented through distortions advanced in the public arena of all types of media, but from the excessive influence of money in campaign politics attempting to fuel voter's attitudes. Simultaneously, our representation in Government has become underserved by the disproportionate, under representation of our fundamental rights. For too many years, our freedom to perform the essential civic duties as intended by our country's philosophical framers, has dismissed neutrality toward the cause of advancing the purpose of humanity. Therefore, our realignment of civic responsibility and virtues must begin the recovery process.

The Founding Fathers of the United States of America created an electoral system of Government as a solution to end violent revolution. This Peaceful Evolution is the Democratic Process we must respect and vote through. While we may not agree with each other, and while we may lose our tempers over years of frustration; violence and property destruction is not a constructive way to improve our cities. Nor should they be used to attract attention in effort to persuade public opinion over differences. Thus, a shift toward responsible discourse through tolerance is essential to our progress. To believe we will succeed, remember the examples set by Marie Curie, Mahatma Gandhi, Amelia Earhart, Martin Luther King, Rosa Parks, Nelson Mandela and countless others who pushed on.

Since the birth of democracy, through the inclusion of term limits and election cycles, elections were never intended to incite violence, but rather to embrace and strengthen the civil side of our human nature. To take responsible action by educating through credible sources of information, is to ensure that fact-based influences conceive our decisions, and serve to protect the pursuit of future happiness. Are we happy in the current state of affairs? Some are, and many are most definitely not. Meanwhile, the violence within the current social unrest caused by centuries of social injustice is not the answer, voting is. Now is not the time for violent Revolution or anarchical chaos, it is time for a chosen evolution based on the strengths of our experiences together, and how we want our memories to serve our future.

Through the race of time that is today's life, we are subjected to forget the original goal of the United States founding philosophies was, and remains to advance human rights:

"WE THE PEOPLE OF THE UNITED STATES, IN ORDER TO form a more perfect Union, establish Justice, insure domestic Tranquility, provide for common defence, promote the general Welfare, and secure the Blessings of Liberty to ourselves and our Posterity, do ordain and establish this Constitution for the United States of America."

-United States Constitution, 1787

Often times, over history, that goal of providing a more prosperous and advanced future has been mistaken as an excuse to spread another global regime. It is understandable why such a foreign perception may exist from some of the influence we have exerted for the world to encounter. The doubt of our fundamental intentions has been reactions to historic actions.

Having lived in the middle east the past two years, I witnessed first-hand how the foreign perception, and trust of the United States has all but irrevocably changed. Resetting the discourse in American politics by driving a healthy conversation geared toward achieving progress, is so necessary, it is common sense. We need to create accomplishments, not political character assassinations resembling school yard bullying. Unfortunately, the toxicity in politics, federal government aside, has set the public's trust of government on fire. But it is a much more personal issue. We know, we are better than this.

The measure of our political experience since 1972 includes the systematic fracture in our politics that has weakened the integrity of public service. While progress takes time and requires patience, we have no excuse other than to move forward.

The virtues, practices and civility of a modern citizen is defined by our ability to adapt, tolerate and overcome adverse conditions by making the most of our time through responsible actions. In the United States, people may represent themselves and independently exercise the freedoms to choose as they live, which is the most essential element of our freedom. But that does not mean we have to tear institutions down to build them up again. Delaying the reach for our greatest potential as we look to build the future, has cost us precious time.

In 1787 during the constitutional convention, Alexander Hamilton, James Madison and John Jay wrote the Federalist Papers to win support for a federal constitution. They published it anonymously out of concern they would be affiliated with the cause as members of the Constitutional Convention. "Publius" translated to "of the people," was their published name and inspiration.

In Federalist Papers 6 & 7, Alexander Hamilton presents with foresight the threat of factions to American Society. He highlights, "*We should be ready to denominate injuries those things which were in reality the justifiable acts of independent sovereignties consulting a distinct interest.*" [2] Today, resulting from prolonged frustrations, left and right factions have evolved from our common frustrations to collide authentic science and history in our mutually shared quest for genuine progress. As provided by constitutionally founded human rights, our technology driven world evolved at light speed while carrying voices of dissent through Freedom of Speech and Freedom of Press like never before. Since the Pilgrims landed at Plymouth Rock on November 11, 1620 and built roads outward, this has been the story of American progress.

Now, in this American moment, and since 2003 through years of political warfare, the influences of political factions have risen to a combative state on the world's main stage. Whether they enjoy reflections of fascist or socialist tendencies, we need to answer eachother in the middle to resolve those obvious issues that divide and prevent us from founding balanced progress.

We have become too quick to dismiss proposals ignited by premature, stereotypical judgement without understanding the deeply born concerns of the accused "neo-fascist conservatives" or "radical, socialist liberals." It is our job as citizens to address this accusatory rhetoric equivalent of school yard bullying and find a middle ground to install a foundation upon which we can all live together, and ensure the continued growth of national prosperity.

Now is the time to enable the government to evolve by our God given right to vote with free choice. In the United States, from the Whiskey Rebellion of 1794 to the 2020 Black Lives Matter movement, we too must decide what is right for our nation to calmly proceed with earned providence toward a solutions-oriented future. Today, through the revolving news cycle of our lives, our attention span has been debilitated and our long-term memory all but erased. Further, we build up heroes as fast as we tear them down. In the public arena, the moment one person does anything in any direction, they will be judged rather than evaluated to be accepted for being themselves. None of us are perfect, but we can try to be. We may retain good intention to embrace living through it.

Our natural tendencies of the competitive spirit have

mobilized progress, but have also intoxicated society through counterproductive negativity, and will continue to disproportionately as long as we fail to right our wrongs. Regardless of entertaining political commentary and the laughs we gain from memes over social media, it is on us, to differentiate between real and fake news since the fake is unlikely to stop despite our best efforts. There will always be the poisonous apple tempting our pleasures to interfere with responsible choice.

Furthermore, let us acknowledge it is our responsibility to recognize how the exploitation of materialism is costing more than our dollars and health: it is costing nature the resources our life depends on. Until we consumers drive industry to adopt more sustainable production methods and materials for our consumption, our progress toward a sustainable future will be delayed, our health will continue to be compromised and our future will remain endangered, as we are... the only human species.

We do not need another Civil War to acknowledge our society's Constitution could use new Amendments to provide additional protections and advances. We certainly do not need another World War for countries to recognize they need to respectfully stop provoking reactions so we can heal ourselves, and the planet we live. From increased storm strength to the prolific amount of ice melting on north and south poles, in addition to the vast scientific data of human impact, we can afford to have a smaller environmental impact.

This request for increased consumer responsibility is not to induce negative economic activity or reduce earning potential. Rather, it is to inspire positive economic outcome whose potential has yet to be realized. This does not have to cost extra, bring a recession or reduce earnings, it is to pivot past-successful industrial models toward creating a new industrial production line that promotes our general health and welfare. Therefore, our individual responsible actions should be evolutionary by our choice to avoid purchasing single use plastic packaging.

Our lives are surrounded by the labor and oil that successfully built our world's industry to present day. We have grown from the land, through its livestock and the corn that more than built our agriculture needs. Today: there is a better way. We possess the technology to enable a better way, but we the people have to take responsibility to respect our property and build an evolved renewable future.

PUBLIUS

❦ 2 ❦

THE COMMON EXPERIENCE

In America, we have all wondered with amazement why many of our easiest common problems just won't go away. From street repairs, to unhealthy fast food, to high rent, to police brutality and inner city violence, our frustration grows as we question why can we not move past the simplest things? We have all witnessed these faults, accused people of ignorance, avoided taking responsibility by passing the buck, or flat our accepted the problems we experience through life as, "it is, what it is." Have we lost our spirit and strength to innovate through challenges and overcome adversity? In the moment, to be honest, it feels like we have, although I will never believe it. Around and round we go like a spin cycle spinning through time, tumbling left over stains on nearly clean laundry into permanence. Instead, from the heat, those stains become more permanent, more more fixed in our favorite shirts and dresses, in society. Whether it is the bleach that burns holes through our general welfare, or the tear that adds character, what is it that really holds us back from truly experiencing *the Great Beauty* of life?

Countless artists, musicians, and authors have expressed challenges, frustrations and provided examples throughout our history of our common, reoccurring challenges. In William Strauss and Neil Howe's books Generations *(1991)* and The Fourth Turning (1997), they theorized and proved their Generational Theory, that many of our deepest challenges are rooted in cyclical history, passed on from one generation to the next as if they are hereditary conditions traveling through our bloodlines.

Unfortunately, I am short on time right now to provide the long list of existent, supporting history that has already been provided. Many of our common problems and frustrations occur because of those dangerous repetitions in the stories of our health, in our mindsets, and through our experiences. Those cyclical challenges have plagued our progress and led to an overflow of frustrations throughout our shared experience that has led to the existential crisis we live in today. Many people have already survived coronavirus and will continue to live through it, but too many have already not.

From Covid's rapid spread to its increasing death toll, to the millions of jobs lost, to the dramatic alteration of students' education, to the inevitable growth of the economic gap between classes that will result in another spin-cycle filled with the pitfalls of generational history... All of this, could have been avoided. Yet, this is not a dark picture, it is an opportunity to recognize that we have a chance to begin fixing us, right now.

If you have trouble believing the above, consider the personal and work related challenges your family has experienced through generations. Think of the cracked roads, collapsing bridges, tainted water lines, and outdated rail systems that paved the way for our personal growth, and commercial trade. Look at our air, our land, our water... and all the problems within the oxygen we breathe, the fire we create, and the water we destroy to realize our humanity's nature enables us to do better.

Through the political nature of today, friends and family are being torn apart, children are being taken away from their mothers by social services in cities and by federal agents at the border. At the end of the day, everyone is just trying to survive, do their job, and improve their family's future with the talents we possess.

Through my own pursuit of happiness, I have always been able to work and socialize, with many friends and colleagues firmly planted in the republican party. Our mutual respect has always been for the person, effort, and shared hobbies, while prohibiting the vicious nature of politics from effecting our friendships. Where friends enjoyed being friends, we like many, have now been drawn apart by the current climate despite our best interests and intentions.

Fairly, due to life's speed as the space between us increased, the frequency of our gatherings grew further apart. We were always more interested in having fun while while sharing how we made lives for ourselves, than talking along party lines or dealing with personal problems. Recently as I shared the stories of my experiences with my dearest friends, the response didn't include questions expressing interest, but rather quickly pivoted toward the political bloodletting of current affairs. While others stayed away from potentially offensive tangents and remained focused on goal-oriented solutions, I felt a deep rift in our individual constitutions had occurred. Why? Never before had reaching the middle in a conversation been so difficult, or so... distracted from making more memories.

In addition to friends, unlike ever before, families have become more divided, and more easily offended, which in turn has prevented healthy conversation concerning the politics of care. From an inability to enjoy their golden years after decades of hard work to create mobility for their families, senior citizens have been stuck in front of the television due to their health risk, with nowhere to go enjoy the fruits of their lives' labor. Instead they watched the country they served and the world they contributed to, begin collapsing alongside their desire to practice the liberty of cherishing every valuable moment remaining...

The 1776 Declaration of Independence begins:

"WHEN IN THE COURSE OF HUMAN EVENTS, IT BECOMES necessary for one people to dissolve the political bands which have connected them with another, and to assume among the powers of the earth, the separate and equal station to which the Laws of Nature and of Nature's God entitle them, a decent respect to the opinions of mankind requires that they should declare the causes which impel them to the separation."

OUR POLITICAL AND SOCIETAL TURMOIL DO NOT REQUIRE militias separate from the United States Government, but rather a realignment, rebirth and re-adoption of our founding common principles. We do not face a similar foreign or domestic threat as our freedoms did 1777 when the Sixth Article of Confederation preserved the right to form militias "unless infested by pirates, but every State is required to keep ready, a well trained, disciplined and equipped militia" which today is the national guard in every state.

At this point in the general election during a global pandemic, our civility is needed to preserve and renew the Liberty and Justice we intend to live in the future and make progress through. Since yesterday, from today and through tomorrow, the morality expressed by our individual actions inspires or destroys the civility that preserves our destiny. The key element to our sustained success has been and will always be, our humanity.

Let us recall the first justification in the 1776 Declaration as stated:

"WE HOLD THESE TRUTHS TO BE SELF-EVIDENT, THAT ALL (*People) are created equal, that they are endowed by their Creator with certain unalienable Rights, that among these are Life, Liberty, and the Pursuit of Happiness - That to secure these Rights, Governments are instituted among (*the People), deriving their just Powers from the Consent of the Governed, that whenever any Form of Government becomes destructive of these ends, it is the Right of the People to alter or abolish it, and to institute new Government, laying its foundation on such principles and organizing its powers in such form, as to them shall seem most likely to affect their Safety and Happiness. Prudence, indeed, will dictate that Governments long established should not be changed for light and transient causes; and accordingly, all experience hath shewn, that mankind are more disposed to suffer, while evils are sufferable, than to right themselves by abolishing the forms to which they are accustomed. But when a long train of abuses and usurpations, pursuing invariably the same Object evinces a design to reduce them under absolute Despotism, it is their right, it is their duty, to throw off such Government, and to provide new Guards for their future security." *(2020 does not require violence or revolution, just elections.)*

"Such has been the patient sufferance of these Colonies; and such is now the necessity which constrains them to alter their former Systems of Government. The history of the present King of Great Britain is a history of repeated injuries and usurpations, all having in direct object the establishment of an absolute Tyranny over these States. To prove this, let Facts be submitted to a candid world."

- Published July 4, 1776

LET US REPLACE THE RIOTS AND RACE ALTERCATIONS WITH voting on November 3rd. Let us hear those facts as the voting electorate of people in possession of common sense. Free from indoctrination or interference, let more people vote than ever before. The word "let" should not be in either sentence for the right to vote is a duty of American citizenship from which we have an oath to protect.

From succeeding past disenfranchisement through Women's Suffrage and the Civil Rights Act of 1964, the right to vote is one men and women have died to protect. Our American Military Cemeteries in the United States, the United Kingdom, France, Belgium, Philippines, Panama, Italy, Solomon Islands, South Korea, Luxembourg, Papua New Guinea, Mexico, Solomon Islands, Gibraltar, Netherlands, Tunisia, Northern Mariana Islands, Cuba, and in Morocco, all speak this truth.

Over the last five years, we have seen the renewal of the women's rights movement that began as early as the 1800s during the temperance movement to free society of alcohol. As mothers to the abolition movement that helped end slavery, and through being the mothers to us all, they should not have had to prove their right to vote. As the female Statue of Liberty stands proud as the love of our lives, let us never forget it is the women who birthed this nation since before Plymouth Rock and encouraged the humanity in our spirit.

Born from the respect of our ancestors, I would like nothing more than to see the energy on the streets and within minority communities pivot their organizational abilities toward considering a proactive solution in creating a citizen-based committee to begin writing a renewable social contract in agreement with America. For future's sake, it is time for us to restore our divine freedoms with responsibility as expressed in our Bill of Rights and in the Constitution of the United States of America. As women exercised their historic responsibility, it would be wise for us to encourage this healthy recycle of history to repeat.

In accordance with Hamilton's *italicized* foresight mentioned above, and in addition to achieving progress on gender equality and balancing the scale of racial justice, the least we can consider doing is to create construction grants toward the physical reconstruction of the urban centers in crisis that often resulted from poor opportunities. For example, inner cities like Detroit deserve to be rebuilt with help from suburban citizens, and granted the safety to provide public service in return. This proposal for public diplomacy is intended to preserve, protect, and advance our union through our shared productive potential.

In the least, an optional budget millage should be present on federal election ballots to allow citizens to volunteer contributions toward the betterment of major cities. If this is not practical for November 2020, then we may consider placing an optional preference box on our 2021 tax returns stating our preferred preference for where our tax dollars are spent. There are needs and necessities determined by the functionality of government, and there are specific areas we wish to improve. This is a simple solution to provide choice and improve transparency.

By reclaiming Life, Liberty and the pursuit of our happiness through peaceful celebration of the upcoming anniversaries for our federal constitution, these can be our accomplishments for a nearly wasted 2020. Let's embrace

Hindsight in 2020 and apply Foresight for 2030. From the wisdom of senior citizens born from the strength of adulthood, to the children in us who are always learning, we are all citizens of the future.

Furthermore, having worked with the press through my public service, I have come to witness the constitutionally guaranteed Freedom of the Press become strained over the last ten years. With the arrival of the 24-hour news cycle, internet news and social media, credible print press has been reduced. To supplement, the freedom of the press on television may consider exercising their freedom to air more positive stories of people's good-doing. This suggestion is merely an attempt to help inspire our pursuit of happiness through positive influence. Freedom of the Press is not for the government to decide. Such would undermine the constitutionally provisioned Freedom of Press we need to preserve for its ability to honorably inform the free world.

The political dirty laundry aired during the national political conventions has ended: now we need to respectfully request campaigns pivot to present their experience-based plans for our future. Do the accomplishments outweigh the grievances and enable a track record capable of paving the way forward? There are more than enough details entrenched in political policy platforms to fill the remaining airtime before 11.3.2020. To be safe in the observation of the campaigns does not make large gatherings of people essential until Coronavirus is contained. Let us flatten the curve over the next 4-6 weeks or until mid-October so it will be safe to vote in person.

Finally, I must re-emphasize the difference between Common Sense 1775 and Common Sense 2020. Common Sense 1775 intended to provoke revolution through the American War of Independence. Common Sense 2020 is meant to inspire a direction toward a Peaceful Evolution through our electoral process that provides choice. Americans long ago established our freedom to choose and we have successfully advanced their original intentions. We do not need digress through more violence from either side.

PUBLIUS

❧ 3 ❧

THE THEORY OF EXPERIENCE

In June 2003, I hypothesized *Experiencism* after witnessing the perversion of politics and government around the second invasion of Iraq. That summer, while taking part in the Washington Semester Program at American University in Washington, DC, there were signs of great trouble ahead. During my previous studies in US History and American Politics at the University of Colorado, I began noticing systematic and societal repetitions conflicting our ability to evolve.

Seeking to study patterns in what I believed to represent cyclical history, I stumbled upon *The Fourth Turning* by William Strauss and Neil Howe where they theorized and provided evidence of cycles in generational history.[1] Reading their conclusion inspired me to look for a solution should our next generational turning be tempted to fail... as it is, today. Hypothesizing the application of "experiencism" as a potential answer in 2003, I realized my theory was too bold to launch without a test period. Out of precaution for others, I tested the theory as I lived my life for the last 17 years. As my thoughts evolved through sleepless hard work and pleasure seeking, it took me around the world 8 times including 93 countries, and through 47 states.

As the freedom of our liberty determines one's ability to respectfully choose how we preserve ourselves to create progress, our liberty also determines our right to live freely within a functioning, naturally progressive society. For example, professionally; I have always been a Progressive Independent seeking the most time efficient solutions applicable through any person.

The timing of this publication occurred at this moment, because we cannot afford to sleep until we generate two categorical breakthroughs. One: where medicine, science and technology produces inventions to solve our medical and environmental disasters. And two: for humanity to restore the promise of our future and its existence by increasing the responsibility of our citizenship envisioned by our country's founders. Through an era of Progressive Modernity, we may successfully enter an Age of Experience during which the combination of our history and science could create success unlike ever before. We have a choice: move forward together, or keep business as usual against the innovative Spirit of America.

Being adopted, I did not know my own history, or what path to explore, so I created my own by learning history, creating experiences, and living through a purpose to help others. Combined with facing relative adversity under the pressure of time, it was not the second road less traveled; but the third I created, that made all the difference in my life.[2] Considering the odds of my adoption in USA 1982 as one of Billions of people on the planet, I remain grateful to live a life that may even help one person.

Today, I believe the path we need to take, is for the global community comprised of every person: students, historians, scientists, inventors, academics, corporations, and in governments - to combine our human experience, and recognize we urgently need to begin a sustainable existence. Such would be a practical application in the study of Evolutionary Political Science.[3]

Having the opportunity to stop traveling after so many years on the road, life took me home to help my parents through Coronavirus and serendipitously offered me an opportunity to finally write this chapter. The surrounding sections evolved from the original premise completed a few weeks ago. Having lived my best life through a theory of understanding purpose and experience for 17 years, the following novel philosophy is offered from my original innovative effort to make a difference through my personal and professional experiences. The hope is to move forward without repeating the mistakes of history past that will continue to plague our future without the intervention of our humanity.

❦

WE LIVE IN A MOMENT OF EVOLUTION WHERE A successful, clear vision of a healthier and more productive future is upon us, but we have not been able to reach our full potential because conflicting interests are stalling progress. While Humanity has experienced tremendous success throughout history, unlocking conscious evolution will break the cycle of generational repetition, and enable a more advanced, harmonious future.

The following introduces my evolved political theory of experiencism, which has since evolved into a philosophy included in the Theory of Experience. Relevant to our time, it is intended to create a middle ground through which advanced solutions may be applied to establish progress and strengthen Humanity.

The Theory of Experience is an existential theory through which human action and decision making is intended to inspire conscious evolution. The practice of *experiencism*, to be an experiencist, or experientialist, is to formulate proactive solutions from one's collective experience in order to enable success while preventing negative events within the destructive cycles of history from repeating. Through this innovative advance of evolution theory, post-modern philosophy, and Darwin's theory of evolution by natural selection, this theory of experience is meant to serve as a theory for self-evolution through which we may progress our human nature. In the following pages, I will explain how the Natural Selection in Social Darwinism may be replaced by Experiential Selection.

The practice of experiencism is to conclude the past, and move forward through an intent to shape the future with the constructive tools that history, science and technology provide. Using the experiences of humanity and its civilization to enable a process of self-evolution may aid in the continuation of the humankind's progress.

Therefore, we may seek a proactive, adventure seeking model of experience to advance decision making by identifying and selecting solutions that promote progress. In order to practice, experientialist decisions may occur after a fully informed and empirically based understanding of history is considered for macro and micro applications to progress and protect our society, economy, and our environment that fuels life. The environmental protection life on this planet requires, fundamentally makes managing climate change a non-political issue. It is our God given right to defend nature, towards nurture.

Through the application of our greatest knowledge, we are individually and therefore systematically capable of determining a stable and advantageous path forward. Locke's empirical process is cornerstone to experiencism but evolves it in contrast by using the sense of experiences to determine solutions through an advanced thought process involving foresight as exhibited by Alexander Hamilton in Chapter 1, the State of Affairs.

Meanwhile, please be advised that the extreme practice of establishing a goal to never repeat yesterday's daily routine, or intentionally avoid life's process and evolution, is unordered and capable of generating chaos for individuals. Please trust that from my personal experience, such is impractical and not a constructive way forward.

This *Policy of Truth* means that our lives possess infinite value through the influence of our life's experience and toward creating the foresight of intent. Although our physical presence on earth ends when our life's clock runs out, our positive influence continues as long as human life continues. If humanity were to parish, one would hope that at least animal species would survive and be able to evolve physically and mentally through time as we have chosen to. How we influence each other passes on through generations, to our friends and family who carry our inherent influence from the lessons of our lives.

Resolving poverty in the United States is as Common Sense an issue as any of our non-political issues. Hoping to put a roof over someone's head, to give them shelter, and a hope that their difficult lives will get better, is not communist or socialist. From the 'equality' mentioned in the Declaration of Independence, to the 'pursuit of happiness' in the Constitution, and through legal protections of the impoverished in due process cases through Constitutional law, resolving poverty issues in the United States is as American as any issue. The eradication of Poverty is also the number 1 priority on the United Nations list of 17 Sustainable Development Goals.

It is clear: to make our streets safer, we need to take care of our own. This same priority applies around the world to Refugees.

We honor the Second Amendment to keep our homes safe when there is no time for police to respond. We know hunting in America is as valuable to our culture that began hunting in Europe after thousands of years of evolution as every species hunts to survive. We love our guns and will not give them up, but we need to use the fire in our hearts to build up those that cannot help themselves. If we practice this approach together, we will make our cities and rural communities safer. Proverbs 14:31 "He who oppresses the poor reproaches his Maker, but he who honors Him has mercy on the needy."[4]

In America, we learned to hunt this land from Native Americans who honored the animal and hunt for all that earth provided their survival. Their religion was to Mother Earth, and Father Sky. Similarly, please consider how much Earth has always provided toward the evolution of our species.

We choose what we eat, we choose how to live, what to grow, what to drive, how to protect our loved ones, and how to care for ourselves and others. Intending to help people is not communist, socialist or fascist, helping through a balance of the achievable, is American and we know we can achieve anything. Yet, homelessness persists as the poverty rate in the United States is 11.8%.[5]

Humanity, through matters of heart, are at the center point for the continuation of species. Our decisions determine whether we evolve or devolve, progress or digress, succeed or fail, or disintegrate into the sands of time. The logical reason behind the process of self-evolution begins with choosing to live for tomorrow by making tomorrow, better than yesterday. "Experiential Selection" is possible when our choices lead to our own progress in mind, body and spirit.

Therefore, 'Experiential Selection' in the Theory of Experiences further challenges Darwin's Theory of Natural Selection considering evolution is based on experiences originating from molecular elements, to organisms, to conscious species, and ultimately through the thought process provided by our humanity. Additionally, Social Darwinism has led to justify racism given the color of a person's skin or physical characteristics enabled the selection of perceived strength and value, versus the realized energy and strength of humans and our humanity, as one species capable of producing its own evolution. Evolution is therefore chosen by conscious decision making through the Element of Humanity.

From in the beginning when Hydrogen combusted on itself long enough to eventually create the oxygen in the air we breathe that fuels our species, millions of years later. As the electrons in elements acted and counteracted, they naturally chose to bond toward benefit, or counteract to create explosive energy. Humans act and counteract similarly to create progress or destruction in individuals, communities, and on a mass scale. After-all, our brains, bodies and personalities are made of the same scientific elements that gave birth to the universe.

I am not surprised by the history of our mixed evolution. As a light bulb turns on through the Tungsten filaments discovered by man, and beneficial x-rays and cancer treatments from radioactivity as created by woman. Categorically, the potential energy of humanity is relative to the combustion of our molecular atoms. This means the Element of Humanity has a naturally occurring place in the periodic table and through Quantum Physics. We discovered it long ago, and now, it will not hurt us to exercise its full potential to create good in the world once again.

The choice we have is to act together toward progress, or counteract each other's best interests, and continue harming people and our planet. Instead of toward death, taxes and destruction that leads to more taxes, this could be an evolution as 1, instead of 50/50. Toward One is the curve we should be increasing provided the increase, will decrease the coronavirus curve beneath flat.

By evaluating recent years up to this moment of evolution: from our counter-actions in the United States through the repetition of aggressive geo-politics, we may conclude that counteractive energy has created another Big Bang moment capable of driving our progress forward... as relative to the creation of the universe in the big bang theory. But now we have a choice over how our elements collide. If we do not choose wisely, this may be our half-life.

The founder of empirical thought John Locke presented in his theory of knowledge, that sense of knowledge is driven by the inspiration to seek pleasure.[6] From our collective experience, it may be agreed that the pain induced by negative outcomes in pleasure seeking, is the beneficial factor of negative experience that provides the educational experience necessary to overcome adversity.

No culture of people should be concerned with losing their way of life. We should all be protecting our lives and preserving our future by ending the pandemics of Coronavirus & Disease, Global Warming & Climate Change, Social Injustice, and to further prevent the political separation from the foundational bedrock of American principle. Regardless of our individual ways and despite our differences, it is the life we have by the air we breathe, and the water we drink that matters most. We shall protect, preserve, and advance their value... without Africa needing plastic bottles.

We have come to a moment of evolution where an evolved Theory of Experience is applicable and capable of facilitating an advanced thought process as desired by the virtues of our nature, for our future.

Publius

❧

DEFINITIONS IN THIS THEORY OF EXPERIENCE
It is by the freedom of one's choice to accept or deny the following:

EXPERIENCISM - A PHILOSOPHY INCLUDING THE STUDY and practical application of empirical experience to learn from, and resolve the past through a natural born strength that carries an intent to shape the future with the constructive instruments provided by history and science. **2.** experiencism is a proclamation theory for self-evolution that qualifies the responsible experience of humanity in civic duty to streamline processes and evolve civilization. **3.** where the scientific empirical process and the evolution of world history join to enable the best future possible. **4.** the Theory of Experience provides an understanding of the value of Time. **5.** applies to the current capitalist economic framework by advancing models of society to generate economic production, eliminate poverty, promote health, and institute global climate management with an intent to stabilize essential life supporting conditions. **6.** as an innovation of empirical thought wherein experience is measured through the senses, experiencism exercises itself as theory of self-evolution capable of converging theoretical science, mechanical engineering, and philosophy as a means for beneficial production.

. . .

EXPERIENCIST - ONE WHO STUDIES INDIVIDUAL, AND collective human experience in history and science, toward the application of gaining experience, to the benefit of an entity capable of self-evolution. **2.** An *experiencist* is capable of identifying problems and applying solutions to one's own life, as well as to entities in an effort to generate evolution toward future societal goals and requirements. **3.** One who is capable of transforming observation into calculated decisions based on the most beneficial outcome. **4.** One who preserves humanity through probability based decisions while considering a possible decision may not be completely favorable. *Actions have unintended consequences, therefore considerate deliberation and calculations must continue toward progress.

EXPERIENTIALIST - A CITIZEN OF THE FUTURE, WHO LIVES their time and experience on a progressive path toward creating evolution **2.** One who carries an intent to learn, educate and apply varieties of experience to strengthen one's community through civic responsibility. **3.** In order to apply one's true potential as part the global community, one possessive of the natural ability to observe action, understand their action will create a reaction, and understand the big picture life offers through the progression of life experience.

❧ 4 ❧

FOR THE WORLD
OUR AIR, FIRE, WATER

Written to advance our progress, the following is a lens through which the conditions of experiencism and experiential thought apply to this moment in history.

❦

From the lessons of our mistakes, failures and gains, the common values in our experience may be applied. To promote our evolution and progress, the world population should choose to exist in agreement, act through mutual interest and toward fair treatment with the fundamental best interest of every inhabitant on our fragile planet.

Our future depends on our ability to embrace successful models capable of resolving issues in our daily lives. This requires connecting to our planet, to generate wisdom we may learn from, and evolve through. By allowing ourselves to learn from, and accept each other, we will become tolerant and activate a care-built world. Meanwhile, the inability to accept, adapt and evolve, is preventing our progress.

28

Recognizing our irresponsible neglect has abandoned the process of our natural evolution, we require an urgent activation of global cooperation to embody the fact we are one human species, responsible for our world, and its future inhabitants...

To apply experiencism, or to be an "experiencist," requires advanced thought to plan, manage, and execute momentum through mindful decision making. To progress through foresight in an effort to avoid repeating mistakes, is to foster an inherent purpose that stimulates progress in ourselves, and throughout society, to solve our most demanding global challenges.

Humanity, like never before, should agree on a course of action to institute solutions and resolve risks to our existence through the practical application of history, science, and technology.

Experiencism applies to the current capitalist economic framework by advancing models of society to eliminate poverty, provide economic health and production, and establish global climate management to institute our stable conditions for life.......

We exist in a moment of evolution where time and progress have stalled. Civilization cannot afford to lose the value of the experiences our history and evolution have produced since the beginning of time. What we do now, will last forever.

Our evolution possesses potential from the strength of our history and through the temple of science to build an innovative foundation for modern society, by working together to design a sustainable, balanced, and progressive existence.

Recognizing a new industrial road can be paved by upcoming breakthroughs in science and technology, will inspire the acceptance and growth of a progressive form of capitalism.

Learning to explore common ground will move us past mistakes, through failures and teach us to advance success.

Developing civic responsibility toward accomplishing our essential goals provides a clean future for the global community to experience...

Our trust of each other is eroded through public distortions and our progress has stalled, while our contributions to society are too few.

United as citizens of the future, and for the world, we can believe in each other by working together for a better tomorrow.

Rule out dangers to our existence by bringing to scale the talents, innovative technologies, and capabilities to invent a modernized, universal civilization...

As soon as we protect future generations by answering their call to change the world, we can emerge from our human pandemic, with the promise of our ancestors in effort to build a better tomorrow.

Initiate World Peace. To reduce emissions and establish a sustainable model for survival, request the United Nations at the this September's General Assembly in New York, to accept a minimum ten-year stop on all acts of war by halting military exercises, international border expansion, production of nuclear weapons, and all provoking actions that could lead to war including international Intellectual Property invasion. We possess the innovative spirit and knowledge to point international defense budgets away from mutually assured destruction, and toward re-inventing our infrastructure. By expanding sustainable intentions and proactive solutions to troubles that lay ahead we, together can write the Art of Peace from the Art of War. The only arms race needed is the race to which country can *breathe* the cleanest air. Imagine what 30% of the international arms production budget would do for the world's infrastructure and employment creation. Manufacturers will not lose opportunity in the quest for sustainability.

Regressive actions must be reversed to set humanity on a united and progressive direction forward to construct the future we were intended to achieve, through the air we breathe...

From the lessons of time, we possess an ability to generate our own evolution, and grow into an Age of Experience, where the sum of our experience creates Time.

Instead of waiting for the next environmental disaster or natural catastrophe to occur, it is on us, to advance past the dangers of our ways, before the damage we create becomes irreversible.

Recognizing the decay of our responsibility, is to regenerate civic duty and advance civility, to sustain global health.

Each of our cultures, religions, and beliefs reach harmony through our shared care and concern, in the fundamental quest to survive on earth's essential elements...

We have reached a breaking point in time that has established an obligation for us to work together to resolve our most pressing issues, and to guarantee our planet has the air and water, we need to survive. Only through our actions can we protect Humanity's only home.

Advancing ourselves and our world through credible information, protects the future of our enhanced knowledge and abilities. We must preserve life supporting conditions, in order to survive.

Through caring for our universally rare water, temperate land, and breathable air, we will employ millennia of history, science, and experience to advance earth's inhabitants.

Experiencism enables progress through a solutions-oriented approach, to grow beyond the cycles of generational history. Socio-economic challenges from race and gender inequality, cannot continue to slow progress. Our equality is the blank slate on which we were born.

Repeating generational history has delayed progress for too long. The balance between humanity, and politics is the middle ground of ideologies, where love provides the stable energy to care. Humanity is the key element to progress in everything.

Publius

The Element of Humanity in the Theory of Experience:

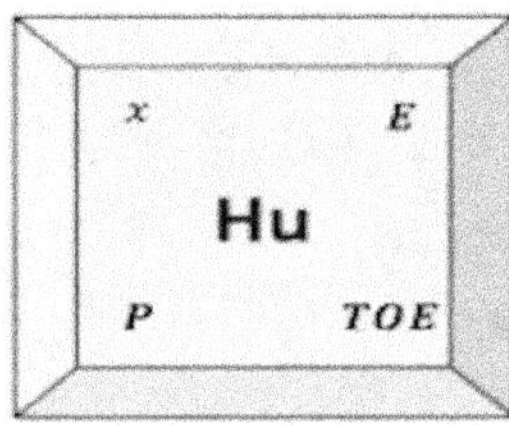

mass number
exponential growth or
decline in mass of People
+/- 7.8 Billion on earth

atomic number
Probability a decision
will induce harm or create
progress: .00 to 1.0

electron charge
Energy of all Relative things
$E = mc^2$

chemical element
Time, Oxygen, Energy in the
impact Humanity has on the
elements of life on Earth.

I HAVE A DREAM FOR...
FOR TOMORROW...

"We all arrived into this world with promise and the potential to succeed. Everything was ours to learn and to experience. Every new skill was a matter of trial and error. How many times did we fall before we could finally walk? No matter the obstacle, we didn't quit. There was a whole world out there, and walking was the only way to reach it."[1] We have persisted since, and how we move into the future from this moment of evolution, will be proof of our courage and ability to adapt as we always have.

When we arrived on our first day in school, we learned so many valuable lessons. We learned to share, we learned to follow directions, and we learned to make friends. As students return to a new mode of school this year, let us envision those fundamental experiences we commonly shared, and what those students are missing as long as our medical, political, and environmental pandemics continue. As we once shouldered the weight of books, let us now carry the weight of our shared responsibility to provide a better tomorrow.

Although the most valuable aspects have of our life's journey has been put on hold, we all have so much to look forward to in renewing the promise tomorrow holds. We have the freedom to make a plan, to determine our dreams, assess our interests, and take stock of our talents. The path of our future, will be one we have chosen." It is relative to our common sense that we know we possess the potential and create the possibility to achieve our true human potential.

When the game is over, even the most competitive athletes playing against one another in the greatest rivalries respect each other at the end of the day for their contribution to sport. Regardless of the color of our skin, or the socio-economic differences we were raised through, we can display tolerance from the respect of the value that each person brings to society.

Students of today, enjoy your youth, but do not betray your goals.[2] Millennials, do not be a lost generation, embody your country's future, it is on us to fulfill our potential. In honor of the lessons of our grandparents, choose to follow in their footsteps long enough to be considered as a next great generation. "People are not excellent because they achieve great things, they achieve great things because they choose to be excellent."[3]

Through good intention, we may achieve excellence while advancing moral intention along the way. Everything starts somewhere...

Whether one collects garbage, washes dishes, goes to school, delivers books; or, one fights fire, protects the law, is a military service member or veteran, we were all intended to respect one another's virtue for the talents they contribute - no matter their role in society. In America, every person possesses a valuable personality, history, and skill that contributes to the greatness of American society and its economy. From dishwashers to farmers to teachers to CEOs and Presidents, we are all people.

Our reality needs to become one where each person plays

a vital role in protecting each-other and preserving the nature of our environment through which we survive. Every American possesses the strength & wisdom through personal experience to see a clear vision of the future from 2020 on. We are proud to be Americans...

To the children who will continue our traditions, please continue to show your care for the earth you will have to raise your families on. For the outdoor playgrounds you cherish, that you will one day hope to share with your own children, please always be learning so you may pass your earned abilities on to future generations. Please choose to do well by your mothers, fathers, families and friends. As past generations have bestowed good intention in us, we also learned to treat others how we want to be treated.

How we live our lives every day and how we choose to treat people close to us preserves civility, and enables the experience we require to succeed. Considering the state of current political affairs, we should begin creating the study of Evolutionary Political Science as a means to travel responsibly into the future. Our story is what will be, History is what was. Good parts preserved, bad parts past. Together, our children can be even more proud of their parents for the roof over their head, clean air to breathe, pure water to drink, and a better planet to live on. This requires believing in each other through the power of love for every species on this planet. Only, we have yet to truly show it.

When we wake up to realize our dreams have not become realities, we get out of bed inspired to seize the day, and tomorrow, for all that it could be. Timeless are the dreams imagined today to be set as goals for tomorrow. Those experiences we have achieved alongside those yet to be seen, are possible through an era of progressive modernity where we embrace every valuable moment this life has to offer, to make the most of tomorrow.

As such, our humanity is capable of transitioning from today's political chaos and into peaceful voting based on the same qualifications we would prefer any employee to have. Our business of helping people, is infinitely more important than who we want to have a drink with. The qualification for this election is simple: Who will be the best President to solve our problems today, and renew the faith in our relationships for a brighter tomorrow? Who are we hiring to run our country?

Regardless of who the next President is, or who the President is now, every American needs to help improve our neighborhoods, communities, and the important multi-cultural society we need to be prouder of. Along the course of American History, we have all seen ups in downs through our lives. Since 2010, we experienced great success and mobility. Now suddenly, nearly 30 million people are unemployed in the United States, myself included by choice to protect my family. Remember before the next pandemic sets in, this all could have been avoidable.

Having lived in the middle east the past two years, I witnessed first-hand how the foreign perception, and trust of the United States has all but irrevocably changed. Resetting the discourse in American politics by driving a healthy conversation geared toward achieving progress, is so necessary, it is common sense. We need to create accomplishments, not political character assassinations resembling school yard bullying. Unfortunately, the toxicity in politics, federal government aside, has set the public's trust of government on fire. But it is a much more personal issue. We know, we are better than this.

Sadly, the measure of our political experience since 1972 includes the systematic fracture in our politics that has weakened the integrity of public service. While progress takes time and requires patience, we have no excuse other than to move forward.

Our cultural understanding of the woes in our society, from racism to social injustice can be brought into simple terms. As of 2018, 38.1 million people in the United States live annually on, or less than \$12,784.[4] In Mississippi, the poverty rate is 19.7%. That means approximately 586,301 persons of +/- 2,976,149 people live in poverty while only 21.8% of persons of ages 25+ possess a bachelor's degree or higher.[5] As hurricanes rage up the Gulf Coast, these people need *shelter from the storm.*

Our progress requires significant effort to assure every American has a roof over their head and may be proud of the life they built. Promoting the mobility of the general welfare of the American population is not socialist or intended to achieve any communist goal or thought, helping those who have less, if they want it, is purely Democracy in Action. If we commit to reducing poverty for whites, blacks, hispanics, Arabs, Indians and Asians, we will reduce crime and make America safer to explore. When we combine all those words together, we are Americans. This is Common Sense.

Remember when Martin Luther King addressed the severity of social and economic conditions in Mississippi in his 1963 speech, *I have a Dream?* Now, 57 years later, Mississippi leads the nation in poverty... and we are worried about improving economic conditions which remains the economic mission of our capitalism as established by Adam Smith in 1759. As an adopted baby from proper Detroit, I can tell you now as an accomplished white 38-year-old: never underestimate the value of putting a roof over someone's head.

The practices of improving our local communities is not socialist by definition in the history of the United States. Promoting the general welfare as described in the United States Constitution and especially in its detailed founding philosophies means the 11.8% poverty rate in the United States is unacceptable.[6]

As our active military and veterans serve honorably, vote from overseas, spend holidays on bases around the world away from their families, and *more* recently lost loved ones while overseas and unable to say "I love you" in person one last time. It is easy to believe we can always do more for our country. Dear friends, please keep your trucks and guns, but please elevate the practice of their existence to be energy efficient through emerging knowledge, technologies and socially sustainable practices in accordance with respecting all our Constitutional rights.

Should we allow the coronavirus, the state of our affairs, the threat of economic turmoil, or the potential disaster from climate change doom our progress? No. To build our future, we need to protect, prevent further decay, and charge full steam ahead as soon as the medical professionals declare it safe. Let's get creative here: the car transportation companies may enable drivers to more frequently courier non-essential goods to peoples homes. Let's give masks, more stay at home, no large gatherings all a 4-6 week chance, see the numbers go down, and not allow this Coronavirus or ourselves to hold us back for years.

Or worse, it unpredictably mutates into a relative of the bubonic plague. That destructive history has already occurred. I don't want to create panic for that is already past, now we have to manage ourselves and our communities. I encourage you to read the similar history of deforestation et al. in advance of the period in European history that took 150 years to recover from. Our four pandemics tell us that we do not have that kind of time to waste, ever. While many countries around the world have reduced deaths and flattened the curve in comparison to the United States, any excuse of low death percentage does not exempt the excuse of any sustained death percentage from Coronavirus, Cancer, Aids, MS, Tuberculosis, Plague, Ebola, Climate Change, Social Injustice, Poverty, Mental Health, Industrial Chemical Waste, Human Destruction, DeForestation... is unacceptable by future standards.

It is common sense that as temperatures rise, more surface water will evaporate in more places, and create more humid landscapes in more places for mosquitos to thrive. We went through Zika virus just four years ago, let's stop Corona's spread before mosquitos again become the next rats to spread disease. Treat the planet as you want Mother Nature to treat you. Together, we have taken on challenges before, we can do it again. It is true our hindsight, that is 2020, provides foresight... toward 2030 and beyond.

Referring to Churchill's quote about not missing a moment from the dismissal of, or omission to prepare in the epigraph: should a future coronavirus be the dimming of the sun, with us not having a way to sustain life on another planet, that will be an opportunity humanity wasted. For distant human space travel to occur, we all have to build for tomorrow while enjoying the fruitful cause of our labor, today.

The answer for our best experienced candidates lies here within. Throughout our discourse in American politics, we have witnessed maturity through our system of checks and balances. Sometimes chosen and sometimes legally upheld by the institutional protections guaranteed by the offsetting roles of the judiciary, the legislative and the executive. The legitimacy of their sustained function was designed to offset abuses of power with an aim to preserve the public's best interest of promoting the general welfare.

Now, the fair and equal representation of the people's best interests are in jeopardy. Voter suppression for political gain remains, again, our most immediate concern. Through world history, while the government's duty to assure the public's safety has too often been fogged by the ambition of power, money, and political gain: We the People must pledge our right to vote is measured as the most sacred exercise of our democracy.

The best candidate in any election in any time through history is the one whose experience is capable of navigating toward progress through the myriad of challenges required to advance the promise of humanity.

As I recognize I may have endangered myself and my future by writing these words, I believe the civic duty of my experience obligates me to serve in this way... for the country that gave me the same opportunity immigrants without shelter, hope for. We cannot allow children to be locked in cages or forcefully separated from their parents. We cannot afford to digress by continuing past mistakes. We can however choose to succeed by enabling experience driven reform toward social, economic and environmental improvement and protection, for all our sakes.

Of the people, for the people, by the people is the cause I attempted to live my life through since being taught "Tabula Rasa" in the 7th grade and upon reading the Constitution in the 8th. Born with an open conscious to learn through experience as theorized in John Locke's 1689 *An Essay Concerning Human Understanding*. It was my birth right to seek experience which led me to vote for, and work for those I believed were properly experienced as a person, applicable to the challenges of the moment. This does not mean I am breaking away from either political party, it just means I am allowed to stand in the middle to make good as I have always tried, and as my constitutional freedoms provide.

From good intention, every action leads to something & somewhere better than before.

If the public health threat reduces, I will proudly wait in

line to vote in person, otherwise I will protect myself and my neighbors by safely mailing in my ballot through the liberty that protects us. As before, my vote will depend on the best history and plans for an administration to create the future as soon as vile propaganda and rhetoric ceases to alter decision making ability.

Remember that in the grand scheme of things: we elect them to office, they do not elect us as citizens. Meanwhile, by way of practicing history, we cannot forget mistakes past because we cannot afford to repeat the negative cycles of history that have plagued us. Naturally, people will always be afraid to encounter change or have to adapt to it. May these last few months be an example of growing pains and not continuing problems to plague us.

Without further dividing our country, let us make this election about fact, not fiction or fairytale, and focus on the business of promoting the general welfare as written in our founding documents. The damage we are creating through the deprivation of our intended unity will be more difficult to repair if we cannot agree our desired future needs to be healthy and sustainable. The *US and Them* mentality can no longer be translated to U.S. and Them, when it comes to the Earth's environment, we are one.

The assassinations of John F. Kennedy, Martin Luther King and Robert Kennedy did far more than just kill men, they killed the progress that cost us 60 years of common sense. Today, we have the economic safety of the emerging industry of sustainable arms where every person's skills and talents are needed to prevent the permanent rise of sea levels and stop the earth from burning. To prevent the assassination of our planet's resources, *we* should take care of our own. Through ups and downs, we will have a prosperous future together.

In what year was the threat of industry induced global

warming first mentioned? Is the thick smog / air pollution adults and children breathe okay? Do we really want to continue living with airborne illnesses, increased medical bills and health conditions including asthma? I've been there, done that, and it is not a good path forward. Clean air, water, and earth to roam is far better. We should be excited for these opportunities, not scared of making our neighborhoods, cities, states and country, an even better place to live. Does it not feel good to help a person, or an animal in distress?

It should be our pleasure filled responsibility to right our wrongs and make Martin Luther King's dream, a reality. Our Common Sense in 2020, is to never stop believing in tomorrow since in many places around the world, today is already tomorrow and they shouldn't have to wake up to our bad news.

It is not hard to understand the current protests as Martin Luther King spoke *I Have a Dream* on August 28, 1963:

"There will be neither rest nor tranquility in America until the negro is granted his citizenship rights. The whirl-winds of revolt will continue to shake the foundations of our nation until the bright day of justice emerges."

Alongside Dr. King's American Dream, Today, I have a belief "this nation" has risen up, and we will begin living out "the true meaning of its creed. We hold these truths to be self-evident that all" *people* "are created equal." To both sides protesting and forming militias, please lay your arms to rest, begin healing our nation and look forward to voting.

Maybe some of us are just born to sing the blues, but we do not have to be without a choice... In honor of Martin Luther King's American Dream:

. . .

"IF AMERICA IS TO BE A GREAT NATION, THIS MUST BECOME true. And so let freedom ring from the prodigious hilltops of New Hampshire. Let freedom ring from the mighty mountains of New York. Let freedom ring from the heightening Alleghenies of Pennsylvania. Let freedom ring from the snow-capped Rockies of Colorado. Let freedom ring from the curvaceous slopes of California. But not only that... Let freedom ring from Stone Mountain of Georgia. Let freedom ring from Lookout Mountain of Tennessee. Let freedom ring from every hill and molehill of Mississippi. From every mountainside, let freedom ring."

While the final fourteen words of his speech are not mine to say, I will say in this moment of global pandemics and at this moment of our chosen evolution: we own the urgent need to calmly balance the scales of justice unlike ever before. We have *again* learned from the Black Lives Matter movement, and will serve to advance justice for all minorities as they were, "created equal" be it that we were born on John Locke's blank slate to experience freedom.

Once we renew the original spirit of the philosophies that created American Liberty, we may choose to adopt a new 28th Constitutional Amendment that should provide Affordable Health Care to every underprivileged population as proposed in 2017. Based on the U.S. Supreme Court case *Helvering v. Davis*, the 29th Amendment should serve as fundamental guarantee our senior citizens receive their already "paid in" social security as appreciation for their years of American citizenship.[7] No one should ever have to live their final days with concern of losing their home.

The 30th Amendment should be written and submitted by the African American community leaders to be ratified alongside the others in accordance with Article Five of the United States Constitution. In the least, such could include state hood for Washington, DC to tribute the ancestors of the slaves who physically built our nation's Capitol (and Capital). Article Five says, "And that no State, without its Consent, shall be deprived of its equal Suffrage in the Senate."

If we can make this election about fact, not fiction, and focus on the business of promoting the general welfare as the founders originally intended, we would honor the effort and memory of those Founding Americans who gave their lives. We do not need revolution, we need peaceful resolve through our elections, and plans to move forward. Without further dividing our country and to prevent the continued growth of instability through despair and poverty, we should make every effort for our Liberty to lead the way through good intentions and well planned actions and solutions. From the lessons of history past, we can live in the present and future together. I pray we can vote peacefully, and united through care as "one Nation under God, indivisible, with liberty and justice for all."

In honor of Publius, Thank you for caring.

Through experience is how I chose to live beginning in the 7th grade, and I remain grateful for every person and piece of history that entered my life. The freedom of our individuality, and one's ability to care, humbles me.

What worked for me may not work for you, but this is again, my best effort to help at this time.

Given the important nature of the moment, I believe this was important for you to consider.

Until we all start helping, some of us will remain *Strong at the Broken Places* but continue *Dancing in the Dark*.[1] [2]

Thank you for reading, thank you for your time.

Sincerely, Jason

Through his commitment to provide public service, Jason Meininger has traveled nearly 1.8 million miles through 47 states and 93 countries studying history, comparative politics and international affairs. A double major in history and polit-ical science at the University of Colorado in Boulder, Jason sought an education from his experiences while focused on applying practical solutions to life around him. In doing so, he has worked alongside U.S. and foreign Presidents, cabinet ministers, CEOs, members of congress in both political parties, and most importantly, people from every walk of life.

Jason was born in 1982 in Southfield, MI. He was adopted at 3 months old and raised in Metropolitan Detroit. His Vietnam veteran father was a tax accountant and his mother an insurance agent. They raised him to have an independent mind, free to make his own decisions, choose his own influ-ences, and learn from his own failures, to a point. Always a student of history, he had no political affiliation until he was 18 upon voting for Al Gore considering he had a more progressive agenda than then Governor Bush.

He attended the University of Michigan in Dearborn for a year before transferring to the University of Colorado - Boulder in 2002. Finding his way into American University's internship program, chance provided fmr. Senator Max Cleland, a triple amputee from Vietnam, as Jason's professor. Still in between political ideologies because of Jason's adop-tion and the abortion issue, he was offended by the failed promises of weapons of mass destruction that led the United States into the Iraq War.

Having been attracted to Sen. John Kerry's experience in April 2003, Jason volunteered to found the Students for Kerry chapter at the University of Colorado. Believing he had not done enough, Jason began driving 20 hours round-trip to Iowa on weekends through his fall semester while listening to class lectures on cassette tape to study.

Volunteering in Iowa resulted in a job offer on the Presidential campaign, and having never worked on a campaign before, it was the opportunity of a life time to supplement his studies with experience. Accepting the job, Jason withdrew from his spring semester of 2004 to go door to door throughout Dubuque County, IA. Then, after living in Fargo for the campaign, he joined the National Advance team which took him through 32 states running motorcades and bus tours including Believe in America: From Sea to Shining Sea Tour.

Jason returned to the University of Colorado to graduate in 2005 before moving to Baltimore to work for then Mayor and future Governor Martin O'Malley before moving again to rejoin Senator Kerry in his Boston office. Seven months later, he moved to Washington, DC to continue working as an aide in the Senate. Having moved 5 times in the first 18 months out of college, Jason spent the next 7.5 years working in the US Capitol hoping to contribute to progress in any way he could. When President Obama won his second term and appointed John Kerry to serve as his Secretary of State, Jason received an appointment to continue as Secretary Kerry's Senior Aide. Jason helped plan, manage and execute diplomatic missions through 83 countries and over a million miles traveled.

Following his time at the State Department, Jason married, and moved to Dubai to work for the next World's

Fair, Expo 2020 Dubai. On March 15, 2020, he urgently flew home to Michigan to help his parents survive Covid-19 through pre-existing conditions. Choosing to be unemployed in order to do so, he has continued providing his brand of public service by attempting to provide masks to his home state, work in green technology, start his own business and write this solution proposal.

The contents of Common Sense 2020 are his own independent conclusions, free from corporate or political direction or persuasion.

REFERENCES

1. THE STATE OF AFFAIRS

1. Paine, Thomas; Common Sense, 1775
2. Hamilton, Alexander; Madison, James; Jay, John; The Federalist Papers (New York: Signet Classic, April 2003) Federalist Nos. 6 & 7

3. THE THEORY OF EXPERIENCE

1. Strauss, William; Howe, Neil Howe, The Fourth Turning: An American Prophecy – What the Cycles of History Tell Us About America's Next Rendezvous with Destiny. (New York: Three Rivers Press, 1997) 123-138, 333-334.
2. Frost, Robert: The Road Not Taken and other poems. (New York: Dover Publications, 1993)
3. Lopez, Anthony & Rose McDermott. *Adaptation, Heritability, and the Emergence of Evolutionary Political Science.* Political Psychology, Vol. 33, No. 3, 2012. Brown University.
4. Proverbs 14:31. Provided by Gideons International Bible, Nashville, TN. Pg. 655
5. United States Census Bureau: Income and Poverty in the United States, 2018. census.gov
6. 5 Locke, John; *An Essay Concerning Human Understanding, Essay 2.* (1689)

5. I HAVE A DREAM FOR...

1. Meininger, Jason: Class of 2000 Commencement Address. Plymouth Salem high school, Michigan.
2. Ecclesiastes 11:9, "Rejoice, O young man, in thy youth."
3. Author unknown. Provided by senior year AP History teacher Scott Beamen, 2000.
4. United States Census Bureau: Income and Poverty in the United States, 2018. census.gov
5. United States Census Bureau: Mississippi, 2014-2018.
6. United States Census Bureau: Income and Poverty in the United States, 2018. census.gov
7. **Helvering v. Davis**, 301 U.S. 619 (1937)

ENDNOTE

1. "The world breaks everyone and afterward many are strong at the broken places. But those that will not break it kills. It kills the very good and the very gentle and the very brave impartially. If you are none of these you can be sure it will kill you too but there will be no special hurry."

    Hemingway, Ernest. **A Farewell to Arms.** New York: Scribner, 1957. Print.

2. Springsteen, Bruce. ***Dancing in the Dark***; Born in the U.S.A. Roy Bittan, Clarence Clemons, Danny Federici, Garry Tallent, Max Weinberg, Steven Van Zandt, Patti Scialfa, Julianne Phillips, et al. Columbia, 1984, Track 11. VEVO through Youtube

9 798868 213845 6